Blueprints Q&A
STEP 2: SURGERY

Blueprints Q&A
STEP 2: SURGERY

SERIES EDITOR:
Michael S. Clement, MD

Fellow, American Academy of Pediatrics
Mountain Park Health Center
Phoenix, Arizona
Clinical Lecturer in Family
 and Community Medicine
University of Arizona College of Medicine
Consultant, Arizona Department
 of Health Services

EDITOR:
Edward W. Nelson, MD

Professor of Surgery
University of Utah
Attending Surgeon
University of Utah Medical Center
Salt Lake City, Utah

Blackwell
Science

©2002 by Blackwell Science, Inc.

EDITORIAL OFFICES:

Commerce Place, 350 Main Street,
  Malden, Massachusetts 02148, USA

Osney Mead, Oxford OX2 0EL, England

25 John Street, London WC1N 2BS, England

23 Ainslie Place, Edinburgh EH3 6AJ, Scotland

54 University Street, Carlton, Victoria 3053, Australia

OTHER EDITORIAL OFFICES:

Blackwell Wissenschafts-Verlag GmbH,
  Kurfürstendamm 57, 10707 Berlin, Germany

Blackwell Science KK, MG Kodenmacho Building,
  7-10 Kodenmacho Nihombashi, Chuo-ku,
  Tokyo 104, Japan

Iowa State University Press, A Blackwell Science Company,
  2121 S. State Avenue, Ames, Iowa 50014-8300, USA

DISTRIBUTORS:

The Americas
  Blackwell Publishing
  c/o AIDC
  P.O. Box 20
  50 Winter Sport Lane
  Williston, VT 05495-0020
  (Telephone orders: 800-216-2522;
  fax orders: 802-864-7626)

Australia Blackwell Science Pty, Ltd.
  54 University Street
  Carlton, Victoria 3053
  (Telephone orders: 03-9347-0300;
  fax orders: 03-9349-3016)

Outside The Americas and Australia
  Blackwell Science, Ltd.
  c/o Marston Book Services, Ltd., P.O. Box 269
  Abingdon, Oxon OX14 4YN, England
  (Telephone orders: 44-01235-465500;
  fax orders: 44-01235-465555)

Acquisitions: Beverly Copland

Development: Angela Gagliano

Production: Irene Herlihy

Manufacturing: Lisa Flanagan

Marketing Manager: Toni Fournier

Cover design by Hannus Design

Typeset by Software Services

Printed and bound by Courier-Stoughton

Printed in the United States of America

01 02 03 04 5 4 3 2 1

The Blackwell Science logo is a trade mark of Blackwell Science Ltd., registered at the United Kingdom Trade Marks Registry

Library of Congress Cataloging-in-Publication Data

Blueprints Q & A step 2. Surgery / editor,
Edward W. Nelson.
    p. ; cm.—(Blueprints Q & A step 2 series)
  ISBN 0-632-04596-5 (pbk.)
  1. Surgery—Examinations, questions, etc.
  2. Physicians—Licenses—United States—Study-guides.
    [DNLM: 1. Surgery—Examination Questions. 2. Surgical Procedures, Operative—Examination Questions.
WO 18.2 B658 2002] I. Title: Blueprints Q&A step 2. Surgery.
II. Title: Blueprints Q and A step two. Surgery. III. Title:
Surgery. IV. Nelson, Edward W. V. Series.
  RD37.2 .B58 2002
  617'.0076—dc21   2001003080

Notice: The indications and dosages of all drugs in this book have been recommended in the medical literature and conform to the practices of the general community. The medications described and treatment prescriptions suggested do not necessarily have specific approval by the Food and Drug Administration for use in the diseases and dosages for which they are recommended. The package insert for each drug should be consulted for use and dosage as approved by the FDA. Because standards for usage change, it is advisable to keep abreast of revised recommendations, particularly those concerning new drugs.

CONTRIBUTORS:

Stephen H. Bailey, MD
Resident, General Surgery
University of Utah
Salt Lake City, Utah

After growing up in Millburn, New Jersey, Stephen moved to Williamstown, Massachusetts to attend Williams College for his undergraduate study. After graduating in 1991, he then earned his medical degree in 1997 from Vanderbilt University School of Medicine in Nashville, Tennessee.

Michelle T. Mueller, MD
Resident, General Surgery
University of Utah
Salt Lake City, Utah

Originally from Littleton, Colorado, Michelle received her medical degree from the University of Colorado Health Sciences Center in 1997. She also spent her undergraduate years at the same University, where she earned a BA in Molecular, Cellular and Developmental Biology.

Clinton B. Webster, MD
Resident, General Surgery
University of Utah
Salt Lake City, Utah

Originally from Midwest City, Oklahoma, Clinton attended the University of Oklahoma for both his undergraduate and graduate study. Receiving a BA in Psychology in 1992, he then entered the University's College of Medicine, where he earned his medical degree in 1997. Clinton now happily lives in Utah with his wife Jami and their new daughter Emma.

REVIEWERS:

Supriya Jagannath, MSIII
Class of 2002
George Washington University
Washington, DC

Brandon Johnson, MD
Class of 1999
University of Alabama School of Medicine
Birmingham, Alabama
Resident in Internal Medicine
Baptist Hospital
Birmingham, Alabama

Donald Yarbrough, MD
Class of 2000
University of Alabama School of Medicine
Birmingham, Alabama
Resident in General Surgery
Mayo Clinic
Rochester, Minnesota

PREFACE

The *Blueprints* Q&A Step 2 Series has been developed to complement our core content *Blueprints* books. Each *Blueprints* Q&A Step 2 book (*Medicine, Pediatrics, Surgery, Psychiatry, and Obstetrics/Gynecology*) was written by residents seeking to provide fourth-year medical students with the highest quality of practice USMLE questions.

Each book covers a single discipline, allowing you to use them during both rotation exams as well as for review prior to Boards. For each book, 100 review questions are presented that cover content typical to the Step 2 USMLE. The questions are divided into two groups of 50 in order to simulate the length of one block of questions on the exam.

Answers are found at the end of the book. Accompanying the correct answer is a discussion of why that option is correct. For longer stem questions, a full discussion is presented covering the individual answers in a combined explanation.

Blackwell has been fortunate to work with expert editors and residents—people like you who have studied for and passed the Boards. They sought to provide you with the very best practice prior to taking the Boards.

We welcome feedback and suggestions you may have about this book or any in the *Blueprints* series. Send to blue@blacksci.com.

All of the authors and staff at Blackwell wish you well on the Boards and in your medical future.

BLOCK **ONE**

QUESTIONS

QUESTION 1

A 39-year-old woman presents to you in clinic for her annual physical exam. She has no medical problems. She takes no medications and has no known allergies. She underwent an appendectomy as a child and is status post tubal ligation. At her clinic visit she is found to have a normal physical exam except that she is hypertensive with a blood pressure of 175/92. She returns for a nurse visit each of the next two weeks where her blood pressure is 180/91 and 179/93. This does not respond to the addition of metoprolol. Six months after adding verapamil she remains hypertensive. The most likely etiology of this patient's hypertension is:

A. Essential hypertension

B. Conn's syndrome

C. Pheochromocytoma

D. Cushing's syndrome

E. Renal artery stenosis

QUESTION 2

The patient is found to have a serum potassium of 2.9. This suggests the diagnosis of:

A. Essential hypertension

B. Conn's syndrome

C. Pheochromocytoma

D. Cushing's syndrome

E. Renal artery stenosis

QUESTION 3

If the patient were found to have a renal vein renin ratio of 1.5, the most likely etiology of her hypertension would be:

A. Renal artery stenosis secondary to atherosclerosis

B. Renal artery stenosis secondary to fibromuscular dysplasia

C. Renal artery stenosis secondary to intimal hyperplasia

D. Renal artery stenosis secondary to Kawasaki's disease

E. None of the above

QUESTION 4

A 55-year-old man undergoes right hemicolectomy for adenocarcinoma. Pathologic analysis of the specimen reveals a 2-cm tumor that invades into but not through muscularis propria, and 0 of 24 lymph nodes have tumor evident on H&E staining. The pathologic stage of this tumor is:

A. A2

B. B1

C. B2

D. C1

E. C2

QUESTION 5

Appropriate adjuvant therapy for this tumor includes:

A. 5 fluorouracil/leucovorin

B. 5 fluorouracil/leucovorin + radiation

C. Radiation alone

D. 5 fluorouracil alone

E. No adjuvant therapy

QUESTION 6

This patient's estimated 5-year survival is:

A. 90%

B. 70–85%

C. 65–75%

D. 45–55%

E. 25%

QUESTION 7

A 65-year-old woman presents to the emergency room with left lower quadrant abdominal pain. T-38.6, HR-85, BP-130/80, RR-14, WBC-15,000. Abdominal exam reveals left lower quadrant tenderness and fullness, but not rebound tenderness or guarding. CT scan reveals a pericolonic abscess around the sigmoid colon. The next appropriate step in managing this patient is:

A. Admit for IV antibiotics.

B. Discharge home on oral antibiotics after IV dose in the ER.

C. Percutaneously drain the abscess and admit with IV antibiotics.

D. Proceed to the operating room for drainage of the abscess and diverting colostomy.

E. Proceed to the operating room for drainage of the abscess and primary anastomosis.

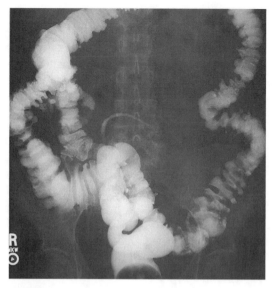

FIGURE 7A

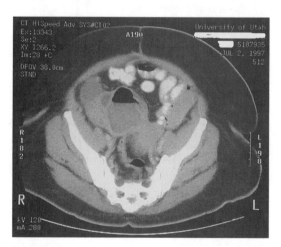

FIGURE 7B

QUESTION 8

All of the following are absolute indications for immediate operative treatment of diverticulitis EXCEPT:

A. First episode in a patient less than 40

B. Continued pain with non-operative therapy

C. Inability to exclude carcinoma

D. Second attack

E. None of the above

QUESTION 9

All of the following are characteristic of ulcerative colitis EXCEPT:

A. Pseudopolyps

B. Confluent disease

C. Thickened bowel wall

D. Frequent extraintestinal manifestations

E. Increased risk of cancer

QUESTION 10

The LEAST likely cause of large bowel obstruction is:

A. Carcinoma

B. Diverticular stricture

C. Cecal volvulus

D. Adhesive band

E. Sigmoid volvulus

QUESTION 11

Which of the following confers the greatest risk of a polyp harboring foci of invasive cancer?

A. Villous histology

B. Tubular histology

C. Tubulovillous histology

D. Hamartomatous pathology

E. None of the above are associated with malignant degeneration.

QUESTION 12

A 3-year-old boy presents to your office with fever and frequent urination. Work-up reveals an *E. coli* urinary tract infection, his fourth in the last two years. You are appropriately concerned about a congenital anomaly and vesicoureteral reflux. The gold standard for documenting reflux is:

A. CT scan

B. Abdominal ultrasound

C. Technetium 99 nuclear scan

D. Voiding cystourethrogram

E. Cystography

QUESTION 13

Vesicoureteral reflux is detrimental for each of the following reasons EXCEPT:

A. Increased post-void residuals

B. Increased renal parenchymal pressure

C. Increased chance of stone formation

D. Easier bacterial access to the kidney

E. Decreased sodium clearance by the kidney

QUESTION 14

A healthy 68-year-old man presents to your office concerned about his urination. He states that his urine is "fizzing" and "popping" before it hits the water in the toilet bowl. He has no other medical problems, has never been hospitalized, has not had prior surgery, and does not take any prescription medications. You suspect that he has pneumaturia. The most likely underlying diagnosis accounting for this phenomenon is:

A. Bladder cancer

B. Colon cancer

C. Diverticulitis

D. Ulcerative colitis

E. Crohn's disease

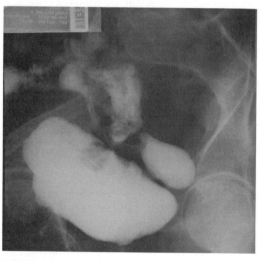

FIGURE 14

QUESTION 15

A healthy 45-year-old man presents to the emergency room complaining of the acute onset of right lower quadrant pain radiating to the groin. He is afebrile and has normal vital signs except for a sinus tachycardia to 110/minute. The abdomen is soft and without localized tenderness. CBC and serum electrolytes are within the normal range. Urinalysis is notable for microscopic hematuria. The most likely diagnosis is:

A. Acute appendicitis

B. Urolithiasis, calcium oxalate stone

C. Urolithiasis, magnesium ammonium phosphate stone

D. Urolithiasis, uric acid stone

E. None of the above

QUESTION 16

A 70-year-old man presents for his annual physical exam. He is in good health with no recent hospitalizations and no prior surgery. He takes no prescription medications and has no allergies. Urinalysis is notable for microscopic hematuria. Cystography is normal. Ultrasound reveals a 3-cm solid left renal mass. The next diagnostic test of choice is:

A. CT scan

B. Selective renal angiography

C. MRI

D. Percutaneous, ultrasound guided renal biopsy

E. None of the above

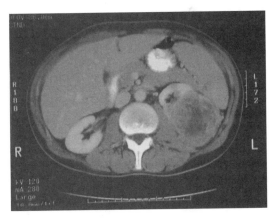

FIGURE 16

QUESTION 17

A 65-year-old man presents to your clinic for an initial evaluation. He has not been to a physician in his entire adult life. He denies medical problems, any prescription medications, or drug allergies. He is 5 feet 10 inches tall, with a 34-inch waist and weighs 70 kg. What is this patient's estimated total body water (TBW)?

A. 35 kg

B. 40 kg

C. 42 kg

D. 50 kg

E. 52 kg

QUESTION 18

Total body water consists of which of the following?

A. Intracellular fluid and intravascular space

B. Extracellular fluid and interstitial space

C. Intravascular and interstitial space

D. Intracellular fluid, intravascular space, and interstitial space

E. None of the above

QUESTION 19

You arrive to take over the surgical ICU service. The first patient presented on morning rounds is a 65-year-old insulin-dependent diabetic, who is seven days status post-elective abdominal aortic aneurysm repair. The patient received a tube graft for this infrarenal aneurysm. His morning labs reveal: Na 150, K 3.9, Cl 106, CO_2 22, BUN 12, Creat 1.5, and glucose 600. The estimated actual serum sodium concentration is:

A. 157

B. 150

C. 142

D. 140

E. 130

QUESTION 20

The estimated plasma osmolarity is:

A. 337

B. 280

C. 356

D. 324

E. None of the above

QUESTION 21

The above patient's measured osmolarity is 300. Which of the following could NOT be responsible for this anion gap?

A. Mannitol

B. Hypertriglyceridemia

C. Ethylene glycol

D. Ethanol

E. Lactic acid

QUESTION 22

Your second patient in the SICU is an 82-year-old, who is seven days status post-elective coronary artery bypass grafting. The patient received seven grafts, which constituted a complete revascularization. The patient was relatively slow to progress after surgery and was extubated on postoperative day 5, with continued moderate (4 liters nasal cannula) oxygen requirements. His morning labs reveal: Na 150, K 3.9, Cl 106, BUN 12, Creat 1.8, and glucose 150. These labs best represent:

A. Increased total body sodium

B. Decreased total body sodium

C. Increased total body water

D. Decreased total body water

E. None of the above

QUESTION 23

Renin is released from the juxtaglomerular cells of afferent arterioles in a response to:

A. Changes in arterial pressure

B. Increase in beta-adrenergic activity

C. Increases in cellular cAMP levels

D. Changes in sodium delivery to the macula densa

E. All of the above

QUESTION 24

Which of the following is NOT correct concerning the renin angiotensin system?

A. Renin cleaves angiotensin I to angiotensin II.

B. Angiotensinogen is produced by the liver.

C. Angiotensin converting enzyme is produced by vascular endothelial cells.

D. One pass through the pulmonary microvasculature converts most of angiotensin I to angiotensin II.

E. All of the above are correct.

QUESTION 25

Which of the following is true regarding aldosterone?

A. It is a mineralocorticoid produced within the zona reticularis.

B. It decreases renal tubular reabsorption of potassium.

C. It acts directly on the distal tubular segments, predominantly the collecting tubules.

D. The net result of its secretion is increased potassium reabsorption and increased sodium excretion.

E. Primary regulation of secretion is angiotensin I.

QUESTION 26

Which of the following regarding water loss is NOT true?

A. Water loss is broken up into insensible losses and sensible losses.

B. Average insensible loss is 10 ml/kg/d.

C. Average urinary loss is 800–1500 ml/d.

D. Minimal urinary loss is 300 ml/d.

E. Insensible losses include skin and intestine.

QUESTION 27

A 65-year-old woman presents to your clinic with a left breast mass she has recently identified. She has a sister with breast cancer and is very concerned that this mass might be malignant. Her last mammogram was several years ago. On physical examination you palpate a 4-cm, mobile, nontender mass. You obtain the mammogram pictured below.

While talking to her you discuss the known risk factors for breast cancer. Which of the following is NOT a risk factor for breast cancer?

A. Family history

B. History of cystic mass on ultrasound

C. Previous biopsy

D. Nulliparity

E. BRCA1

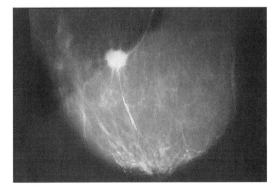

FIGURE 27

QUESTION 28

The most appropriate next step in this patient's work-up is:

A. Biopsy

B. Chest x-ray

C. BRCA1 genetics

D. A and B

E. None of the above

QUESTION 29

The biopsy result comes back positive for invasive ductal adenocarcinoma. You refer her to a general surgeon for mastectomy. All of the following factors will help predict this patient's risk of recurrence EXCEPT:

A. Estrogen receptor and progesterone receptor status

B. Tumor size

C. Histologic grade

D. Age

E. Flow cytometry

QUESTION 30

The patient undergoes a modified radical mastectomy. Pathologic evaluation of the specimen reveals a 6-cm tumor with 4 of 26 axillary nodes positive for tumor on H&E staining. What is the stage of her disease?

A. Stage I

B. Stage IIA

C. Stage IIB

D. Stage IIIA

E. Stage IIIB

QUESTION 31

Screening mammography has been shown to reduce breast cancer mortality by identifying early nonpalpable lesions. All of the following characteristics found on mammograms are suspicious for malignancy EXCEPT:

A. Densities with smooth margins

B. Spiculated lesions

C. Microcalcifications

D. Rod-like branching patterns

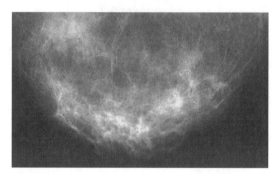

FIGURE 31

QUESTION 32

A 35-year-old woman comes to your office with concerns of a right breast mass. This mass is tender and appears to feel bigger and smaller at various times. On examination you are able to palpate several areas of thickened breast tissue in both breasts. The most likely diagnosis is:

A. Mondor's disease

B. Duct ectasia

C. Fibrocystic change

D. Fibroadenoma

E. None of the above

QUESTION 33

A 36-year-old male comes to you complaining of an increase in bilateral breast tissue. Possible causes for this are:

A. Spironolactone

B. Deficient androgens

C. Deficient estrogens

D. A and B

E. All of the above

QUESTION 34

The lymphatic drainage of the breast travels along the axillary vein and medially to the internal mammary nodes. Which of the following statements regarding nodes is NOT true?

A. The level is based on the relationship between the nodes and the pectoralis minor muscle.

B. Level one nodes are medial to the muscle.

C. Level two nodes are beneath the muscle.

D. Level three nodes are medial to the muscle.

QUESTION 35

A 57-year-old woman is referred to you for a 5-cm left breast mass. She has had a mammogram within the last year. A biopsy is performed that revealed ductal carcinoma *in situ*. After a discussion with you, she decides to undergo a mastectomy.

Post-operatively she is doing well except for weakness of the serratus anterior muscle. Which nerve was damaged during the mastectomy?

A. Thoracodorsal nerve

B. Long thoracic nerve

C. Intercostobrachiocutaneous nerve

D. Subscapular nerve

QUESTIONS 36–39

Match the chemotherapeutic agent on the left with the most appropriate description.

36. Mitotic spindle inhibitor   A. Bleomycin

37. Platinum coordination compound   B. Cis-platinum

38. Dose-related pulmonary fibrosis   C. Taxol

39. Non-steroidal antiestrogen   D. Tamoxifen

QUESTION 40

A 42-year-old obese woman presents to your clinic with a 2-year history of intermittent right upper quadrant pain that often begins after eating a meal and subsides over several hours. You suspect biliary colic. Gallstones are composed of all of the following EXCEPT:

A. Bile salts

B. Free fatty acids

C. Lecithin

D. Cholesterol

QUESTION 41

A 50-year-old male, with past medical history significant only for ulcerative colitis, presents to your office. He complains of right upper quadrant pain, pruritus, fever, fatigue, and a 10-pound weight loss in the last six months. In addition, he states that he has intermittent episodes of "turning yellow." He underwent definitive surgical treatment for his ulcerative colitis over 15 years ago.

The most likely diagnosis is:

A. Pancreatic cancer

B. Primary sclerosing cholangitis

C. Cholelithiasis

D. Bile duct stricture from previous surgery

E. Hepatocellular carcinoma

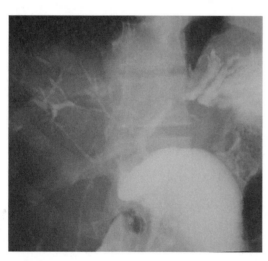

FIGURE 41

QUESTION 42

The gold standard test performed in order to make this diagnosis is:

A. CT scan of the abdomen

B. ERCP

C. Selective angiography

D. Exploratory laparotomy

E. PET scan

QUESTION 43

A 70-year-old diabetic male presents to the emergency room with a history of rapid onset of severe abdominal pain, nausea, and vomiting. T-36.0, RR-26, HR-110, BP-115/80. As part of your work-up you obtain these abdominal films:

The diagnosis that is most consistent with this x-ray is:

A. Emphysematous cholecystitis

B. Peptic ulcer disease

C. Gastric carcinoma

D. Small bowel obstruction

E. Pancreatic pseudocyst

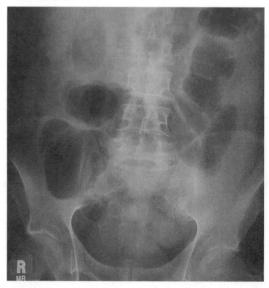

FIGURE 43

QUESTION 44

The bacteria most commonly cultured in this condition is:

A. *Clostridium perfringens*

B. *E. coli*

C. *Klebsiella pneumoniae*

D. *Enterobacter cloacae*

E. *Staphylococcus aureus*

QUESTION 45

A 38-year-old restrained female driver is involved in a motor vehicle crash. She was transported by ground, hemodynamically stable, and neurologically intact. Physical exam reveals no obvious external trauma. She received an abdominal CT scan that was without abnormality other than gallstones noted within the gallbladder. There is no other pathology. During recovery from her accident the patient denies any symptoms of cholelithiasis. The next step in management of this problem is:

A. Return for elective laparoscopic cholecystectomy

B. Chenodeoxycholic acid

C. Percutaneous transhepatic cholecystolitholysis

D. No treatment

E. Elective laparoscopic cholecystectomy prior to discharge

QUESTION 46

She returns to your clinic six months later. She states that she has had 4–5 episodes of right upper quadrant abdominal pain after eating a big meal. Her most recent episode was two nights ago, and the pain was so severe that she required narcotics in the emergency room. The pain is rapid in onset, cramping in character, and abates over several hours. You suspect these symptoms are secondary to her gallstones. The most appropriate way to manage this patient is:

A. Laparoscopic cholecystectomy

B. Continued expectant management and cholecystectomy if cholecystitis develops

C. ERCP to evaluate for common duct stones

D. Treatment with chenodeoxycholic acid

E. Treatment with nafcillin

QUESTION 47

A 3-week-old infant is referred to you for evaluation of a giant congenital nevus. The parents are concerned about the chance of cancer in this lesion. Which one of the following is NOT true regarding giant congenital nevi?

A. The incidence of malignant change is 1–2%.

B. A nevus covering the entire nose is considered "giant."

C. The malignant tumors that form in these nevi are usually melanoma.

D. They tend to dramatically regress with age.

QUESTION 48

An 80-year-old man is in your clinic complaining of multiple skin lesions. These lesions are elevated, dark black, with a waxy creased surface. The most likely diagnosis is:

A. Melanoma

B. Spitz nevus

C. Seborrheic keratoses

D. Basal cell carcinoma

QUESTION 49

You see a 65-year-old woman with pink scaly lesions on her hands and face consistent with actinic keratosis. Which of the following is NOT correct about actinic keratoses?

A. These lesions can become hyperkeratotic.

B. The malignant potential is 1/1,000 to squamous cell carcinoma.

C. These lesions do not regress spontaneously.

D. All of the above are correct.

E. None of the above are correct.

QUESTION 50

You see a 69-year-old man in your office who has had several basal cell cancers removed in the past and most likely has another lesion on his forehead today. Which of the following is not a risk factor for basal cell carcinoma?

A. Sun exposure

B. Male sex

C. Increased skin pigmentation

D. Burn scars

E. Immunosuppression

BLOCK **TWO**

QUESTIONS

QUESTION 51

A 16-year-old male comes to your office and tells you that he has a family history of dysplastic nevi. Which of the following is NOT true?

A. Patients with family history of dysplastic nevi have an increased risk of melanoma.

B. Dysplastic nevi have fuzzy borders and are frequently variegated.

C. A target shape pattern is classic for dysplastic nevi.

D. Patients should be examined every 3–12 months.

E. All dysplastic nevi should be removed.

QUESTION 52

A 65-year-old man presents to the emergency room having had an episode of vomiting bright red blood. The most common cause of active upper gastrointestinal bleeding with hematemesis is:

A. Esophageal varices

B. Peptic ulcer disease

C. Mallory-Weiss tear

D. Gastritis

E. None of the above

QUESTION 53

The patient continues to have multiple episodes of bleeding in the emergency room. Upper endoscopy reveals an actively bleeding duodenal ulcer. Cautery and sclerotherapy are unable to control the bleeding. T-37, HR-95, BP-110/80, RR-16. The most appropriate next step in the management of this problem is:

A. Urgent exploratory laparotomy

B. Admit to the ICU for fluid resuscitation and fresh frozen plasma.

C. Insert esophageal balloon to tamponade the bleeding.

D. Urgent exploratory laparoscopy

E. None of the above

QUESTION 54

The most appropriate first maneuver after entering the abdomen is:

A. Cross clamp the aorta

B. Dissect out the celiac axis to obtain easy vascular control

C. Duodenotomy, suture the ulcer base to ligate the gastroduodenal artery

D. Duodenotomy, suture ulcer base to ligate common duodenal artery

E. Manually compress the aorta to obtain vascular control.

QUESTION 55

A 65-year-old man presents to your office because his daughter noticed that he appeared yellow. On further questioning, he notes that he has had a decreased appetite and has lost 15 pounds over three months. He has a remote history of smoking but is otherwise healthy and vigorous. His exam is unremarkable except for marked scleral icterus. After obtaining serum chemistries, your next diagnostic step should be:

A. CT scan of the abdomen

B. EGD

C. ERCP

D. PET scan

E. None of the above

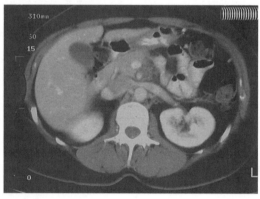

FIGURE 55

QUESTION 56

The periampullary tumor with the LEAST favorable prognosis is:

A. Pancreatic adenocarcinoma

B. Ampullary adenocarcinoma

C. Cholangiocarcinoma

D. Duodenal adenocarcinoma

E. None of the above

QUESTION 57

Which of the following has NOT been epidemiologically linked to pancreatic adenocarcinoma?

A. Cigarette smoking

B. Alcohol consumption

C. Organic solvents

D. Nitrates

E. Petroleum products

QUESTION 58

A 45-year-old woman is referred to your office because she has hypoglycemic symptoms that are relieved with glucose intake and she has a fasting blood sugar of 40. You suspect a pancreatic tumor. The neoplastic cell type accounting for this syndrome is:

A. Alpha cell

B. Beta cell

C. D cell

D. PP cell

E. None of the above

QUESTION 59

A 65-year-old alcoholic presents to the emergency room with severe abdominal pain of 24 hours duration. His sister tells you that he went on a three-day drinking binge about five days ago. His abdomen is diffusely tender. T-38.8, HR-110, BP-120/90, RR-24, WBC-22,000 blood glucose-260, SGOT-400, LDH-400, and amylase-350. You admit the patient to the ICU and begin your resuscitation of the patient's acute pancreatitis. On hospital day 2, the hematocrit has fallen from 50 to 30, BUN has risen from 20 to 30, pO_2 is 55 on 90% FiO_2, the base deficit is −9 and the patient has received 30 liters of fluid while making 2000 cc of urine since admission. Serum calcium is 8.9. The best estimate of the patient's mortality is:

A. 20%

B. 40%

C. 60%

D. 80%

E. 100%

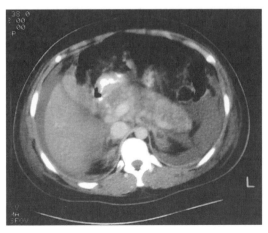

FIGURE 59

QUESTION 60

A 72-year-old man was involved in a high-speed motor vehicle crash and complains of right hip pain. You suspect the most common type of hip dislocation because on exam you note:

A. External rotation

B. Internal rotation

C. External rotation with foreshortening

D. Internal rotation with foreshortening

E. None of the above

QUESTION 61

A 39-year-old woman presents to your office complaining of mild to moderate intermittent abdominal pain and a sense of depression. She is otherwise healthy and her only prior hospital admission was for a kidney stone, which passed spontaneously. You are concerned about hypercalcemia. Which of the following is NOT a cause of hypercalcemia:

A. Hyperparathyroidism

B. Hyperthyroidism

C. Sarcoidosis

D. Hydrochlorothiazide

E. All of the above are causes of hypercalcemia.

QUESTION 62

The patient has serum calcium of 12.8 and an elevated PTH level. Which of the following tests must be obtained prior to proceeding to the operating room?

A. CT scan

B. Ultrasound

C. Sestamibi scan

D. MRI

E. None of the above

QUESTION 63

A 26-year-old student presents to your office complaining of occasional painful swelling in his right groin. This pain occurs after vigorous activity and then abates. You confirm an indirect inguinal hernia with the appropriate physical exam. Which of the following statements are true regarding groin hernia?

A. They occur more commonly in African-Americans than Caucasians.

B. They occur most commonly in the femoral canal.

C. They most often present with incarceration.

D. They are uncommon in children.

E. None of the above

QUESTIONS 64–68

Match the following hernias with the correct definition.

64. Through Hesselbach's triangle   **A.** Indirect hernia

65. Through the inguinal canal   **B.** Direct hernia

66. Hernia with a Meckel's diverticulum   **C.** Richter's hernia

67. Hernia through the linea semilunaris   **D.** Littre's hernia

68. Hernia with a knuckle of bowel   **E.** Spigelian hernia

QUESTION 69

Which of the following is INCORRECT with regard to melanoma?

A. It most often arises from a pre-existing mole.

B. It is highly curable if the depth of invasion is less than 0.75 mm.

C. Staging is usually performed with the sentinel node technique.

D. Skin grafts are usually required to cover the wound after excision.

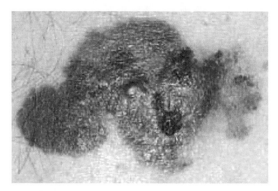

FIGURE 69

QUESTION 70

A 52-year-old white male presents to your office with the primary complaint of painful and difficult swallowing. He is moderately obese and his medical history is notable for hypertension, remote appendectomy, and he is an active one-pack per day smoker for 30 years.

After obtaining a complete history and physical, the most appropriate first diagnostic study to obtain is:

A. EGD

B. CT scan of the chest

C. Great vessel angiography

D. Barium swallow

E. Serum CEA

QUESTION 71

Upper endoscopy is obtained that reveals confluent velvety-appearing changes at the GE junction. Biopsy reveals goblet cells. This most likely represents:

A. Barrett's esophagus

B. Candida esophagitis

C. Mallory–Weiss tear

D. Gastric carcinoma

E. Esophageal stricture

QUESTION 72

The best initial therapy listed for this condition is:

A. Acid suppression

B. Referral for laparoscopic Nissen fundoplication

C. YAG-laser ablation

D. Esophagogastrectomy

E. 12-month surveillance EGD

QUESTION 73

A 60-year-old male is evaluated in your office. He complains of difficulty swallowing and severe pain while swallowing. Barium swallow is shown below.

The most likely diagnosis is:

A. Diffuse esophageal spasm

B. Nutcracker esophagus

C. Achalasia

D. Esophageal diverticula

E. Esophageal carcinoma

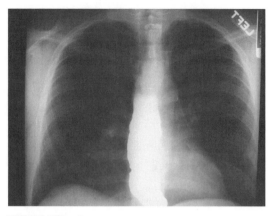

FIGURE 73B

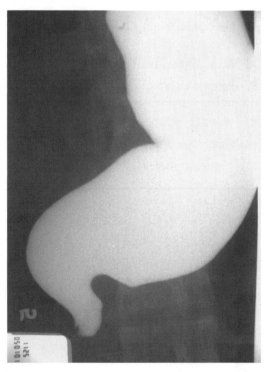

FIGURE 73A

QUESTION 74

The best therapy listed for this condition is:

A. 12 weeks of H2 blocker therapy

B. Laparoscopic Nissen fundoplication

C. Heller myotomy

D. Esophagogastrectomy

E. Esophageal diverticulectomy

QUESTION 75

A 4-year-old is brought to the emergency department by his parents after having thought to have digested liquid drain opener (liquid alkali). The child is crying aggressively but has no obvious injury to the mouth or pharynx.

Appropriate initial therapy consists of:

A. Dilution of the alkali with copious oral intake

B. Immediate induction of vomiting

C. Discharge from emergency department since there is no obvious evidence of ingestion

D. Close observation in the emergency department for airway obstruction

QUESTION 76

If this child did ingest liquid drain opener, he will require all of the following EXCEPT:

A. Immediate EGD to assess degree of burn

B. Broad-spectrum antibiotics once injury is confirmed

C. Water soluble esophagography followed by dilute barium to evaluate for esophageal perforation

D. Long term follow-up to evaluate for strictures

E. All of the above are necessary

QUESTION 77

A 65-year-old man presents to your office after having upper endoscopy for symptoms of gastroesophageal reflux disease. He was found to have Barrett's esophagus and is concerned about the potential that he may now have or may develop cancer. You have a discussion with him about a variety of esophageal conditions and tell him that each of the following is a premalignant esophageal lesion EXCEPT:

A. Barrett's esophagus

B. Caustic stricture

C. Plummer–Vinson syndrome

D. Boerhaave's syndrome

QUESTION 78

A 76-year-old man presents to your office complaining of frequent regurgitation of undigested food and chest pressure after eating. This regurgitation is effortless. You suspect an esophageal diverticulum. Most esophageal diverticula are caused by:

A. Elevated intraluminal pressures

B. Malignant invasion

C. Congenital malformation

D. Iatrogenic investigation

E. DCC mutation

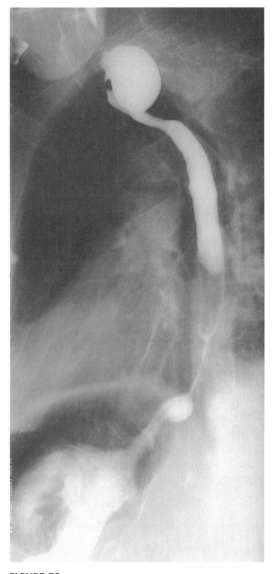

FIGURE 78

QUESTION 79

A 46-year-old man with end-stage renal disease, hypertension, peripheral vascular disease, and coronary artery disease, who is two years status post-cadaveric renal transplant, presents to your office with complaints of pain in his throat. This pain is exacerbated by oral intake. He was recently hospitalized for an episode of rejection. You suspect that his pain may be due to esophagitis. The most likely source of infectious esophagitis in this patient is:

A. Herpes simplex virus

B. Syphilis

C. Mycobacteria

D. Protozoa

E. Candida

QUESTION 80

You are called to the PACU to see your postoperative patient. She is a 76-year-old white female, who has just undergone laparoscopic cholecystectomy. She is poorly responsive. Her current vital signs are: T-37.5, HR-120, BP-98/64, RR-8, and she has an O_2 saturation of 80% on 40% Face mask. Her arterial blood gas is pH 7.29, pCO_2 55, pO_2 35, HCO_3 25.4.

This blood gas is most consistent with:

A. Uncompensated metabolic acidosis

B. Uncompensated respiratory acidosis

C. Compensated metabolic acidosis

D. Compensated respiratory acidosis

QUESTION 81

The most appropriate next step in the management of this patient is:

A. Emergent return to the operating room for treatment of abdominal perforation

B. Emergent reintubation by the anesthesiologist

C. Nothing, the patient will blow off the excess CO_2 from the abdominal insufflation within 2 minutes.

D. Administration of naloxone

QUESTION 82

The most appropriate reason for her to be monitored in the ICU is:

A. Despite normal chest x-ray and EKG, all elderly patients with dyspnea require monitoring in the ICU.

B. She has suffered an acute myocardial infarction secondary to hypoxia.

C. She has advanced pulmonary disease.

D. She requires treatment for her pneumothorax.

E. She does not need to be monitored in the ICU.

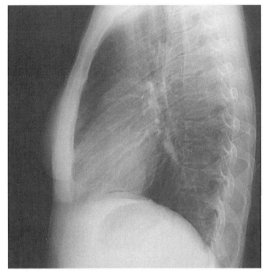

FIGURE 82B

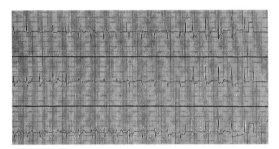

FIGURE 82A

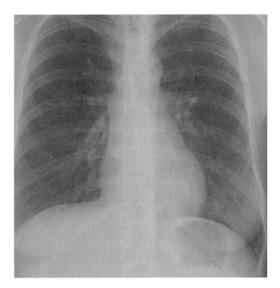

FIGURE 82C

QUESTION 83

A 70-year-old female is returned to the surgical ICU for hypotension and mental status changes. She is seven days post-op from an AVR/CABG. Vital signs are: T-38.1, HR-115, BP-90/40, RR-30. She is in respiratory failure and is reintubated by you upon arrival. EKG reveals a left bundle branch block that was present preoperatively. You place a PA catheter and the following numbers are obtained:

Cardiac index 5.2, CVP 10, PCWP 10, SVR 325.

These PA catheter readings are consistent with:

A. Cardiogenic shock

B. Septic shock

C. Hemorrhagic shock

D. Neurologic shock

E. Improper location of catheter

QUESTION 84

The most appropriate next step in the management of this patient is:

A. Start dopamine to improve blood pressure and cardiac output.

B. Administer a beta blocker to protect the heart from an evolving infarction.

C. Administer crystalloid to improve preload and increase mean arterial pressure.

D. Place intra-aortic balloon pump to assist with mean arterial pressure and coronary artery perfusion.

QUESTION 85

Troponin levels and chest x-ray are normal. LFTs are obtained, which are as follows: Total bilirubin 4.0, ALT 460, AST 378, Alk Phos 551, and amylase 200. You obtain an abdominal ultrasound and HIDA scan.

The most likely cause for this patient's deterioration is:

A. Fulminant hepatic failure

B. Perforated peptic ulcer

C. Pseudomembranous colitis

D. Acalculous cholecystitis

E. Pancreatitis

QUESTION 86

You are taking over the ICU service and your first patient is a 76-year-old female who is three days status post-gastric resection for a perforated gastric ulcer. Her perioperative course was complicated by emesis and aspiration that has yielded a florid pneumonia requiring significant ventilator support. You suspect that she will have an extended ICU stay. The most effective form of nutrition in this patient is:

A. D10 ½ normal saline with 20 meq KCl

B. Total parenertal nutrition

C. Enteral nutrition per nasoenteric tube

D. D5 ½ normal saline with 20 meq KCl + a multivitamin supplement

E. Most intubated patients do not require early nutrition. Enteral nutrition should be started at post-operative day 7.

QUESTION 87

The patient in the previous scenario has decreasing oxygen saturations and pO_2. You make sure that there is not a mucus plug with lobar collapse or pneumothorax by obtaining an x-ray, which reveals diffuse bilateral infiltrates consistent with progressing acute lung injury. Maneuver(s) that you can employ to improve oxygenation include:

A. Increasing FiO_2

B. Decreasing PEEP

C. Adding an inspiratory pause

D. Increasing tidal volume

E. Increasing PEEP

QUESTION 88

The next morning you check a repeat x-ray on this patient and are concerned that her endotracheal tube has moved. The proper position of an endotracheal tube as seen on chest x-ray is:

A. At the level of the sternal notch

B. 1–2 cm above the carina

C. 1–2 cm below the carina

D. At the level of the aortic arch

E. Within the hypopharynx

QUESTION 89

Later in the day your patient is found to have the following arterial blood gas: 7.25/60/85. You want to correct her respiratory acidosis. Which intervention will change minute ventilation the most with the smallest corresponding increase in dead space ventilation?

A. Increasing PEEP

B. Increasing ventilatory rate

C. Increasing tidal volume

D. Decreasing PEEP

E. Decreasing tidal volume

QUESTION 90

The chest x-ray shown below is consistent with:

A. Pneumothorax

B. Pneumonia

C. Right main stem intubation

D. Tamponade

E. Pulmonary edema

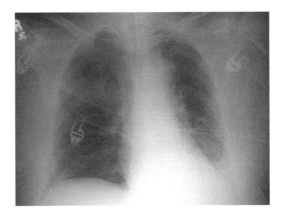

FIGURE 90

QUESTION 91

A 35-year-old woman presents to your office complaining of decreased energy level, thinning hair, cold intolerance, and a general malaise. You are concerned that she might be hypothyroid. Which of the following systems is NOT affected by thyroid hormone?

A. Development

B. Cardiovascular

C. Endocrine

D. Hematopoiesis

E. None of the above

QUESTION 92

The C cells of the thyroid secrete calcitonin. Which of the following is NOT a function of calcitonin?

A. Enhances osteoclastic bone resorption

B. Inhibits osteoclastic bone resorption

C. Inhibits renal calcium excretion

D. A and B

QUESTION 93

You see a 49-year-old male in clinic who comes to you complaining of weight gain and feeling tired. You obtain a TSH, which is elevated. Which of the following is NOT a cause of hypothyroidism?

A. Hashimoto's thyroiditis

B. Graves' disease

C. Iodine deficiency

D. Prior thyroid surgery

QUESTION 94

A 31-year-old woman presented to your office concerned about a lump in her throat. You were able to palpate a dominant thyroid nodule. You obtained a fine needle aspirate of the nodule that revealed definitively benign pathology. The most appropriate next step in the management of this problem is:

A. TSH suppression

B. Enucleation

C. Total thyroidectomy

D. Partial thyroidectomy

E. No further treatment

QUESTION 95

You see a 40-year-old woman with a dominant thyroid nodule. Fine needle aspirate is indeterminate. You take her to the operating room for thyroidectomy. Which of the following statements is INCORRECT?

A. Arterial supply to the thyroid is from the superior, middle, and inferior thyroid arteries.

B. Venous drainage is from the superior, middle, and inferior thyroid veins.

C. The right recurrent laryngeal nerve loops around the subclavian.

D. The left recurrent laryngeal nerve loops around the aortic arch.

QUESTION 96

You see a 61-year-old man in clinic referred to you for the management of asymptomatic hypercalcemia. He was noted to have an elevated calcium (10.9) on a routine lab draw. Which of the following is NOT a cause of hypercalcemia?

A. Multiple myeloma

B. Milk–alkali syndrome

C. Paraneoplastic syndrome

D. Familial hypocalcemic hypercalcuria

QUESTION 97

You see a 34-year-old man in clinic who complains of nausea, vomiting, muscle weakness, and a history of renal stones. After checking a PTH, you diagnose him with hyperparathyroidism. Which of the following symptoms is NOT associated with hyperparathyroidism?

A. Increased appetite

B. Brown tumors

C. Skin pruritus

D. Heart block

QUESTION 98

You see a 50-year-old woman who you think has primary hyperparathyroidism. In working her up you must check which of the following?

A. Serum calcium and PTH

B. 24 hours urinary calcium

C. Calcium/creatinine clearance ratio

D. Bone densitometry

QUESTION 99

You see a patient with parathyroid hyperplasia, medullary carcinoma of thyroid, and pheochromocytoma. This constellation of diagnoses represents which syndrome?

A. MEN I

B. MEN IIA

C. MEN IIB

D. None of the above

QUESTION 100

An 18-year-old boy presents to the emergency room complaining of abdominal pain. His syndrome began 18 hours ago with nausea and decreased appetite followed by vomiting. He then developed a difficult to localize central abdominal pain followed by pain localizing to the right lower quadrant. T-38.5, RR-12, HR-70, BP-110/80, WBC-11, urinalysis-normal, amylase-60. On exam the patient has focal right lower quadrant tenderness. The most appropriate next step in the management of this patient is:

A. Proceed to the operating room.

B. Ultrasound

C. CT scan

D. HIDA scan

E. Abdominal x-ray series

QUESTION 101

The most likely diagnosis is:

A. Cholecystitis

B. Appendicitis

C. Small bowel obstruction

D. Pancreatitis

E. Gastroenteritis

BLOCK **ONE**

ANSWERS

ANSWER 1

A.

ANSWER 2

B.

ANSWER 3

B. This young woman has refractory hypertension that must be worked up further. While the most likely cause remains essential hypertension, there are several surgically correctable sources of hypertension that must be considered.

Conn's syndrome is characterized by hypertension secondary to hyperaldosteronism arising from an adrenal tumor or adrenal hyperplasia. Serum potassium is a good screening test for this phenomenon. Hyperaldosteronism causes significant hypokalemia. If a patient does not have hypokalemia, the diagnosis of Conn's syndrome can be ruled out. Seventy percent of patients with Conn's syndrome have an adrenal adenoma, while 30% have epithelial hyperplasia. Adrenocortical carcinoma is an exceptionally rare cause of hyperaldosteronism. Symptoms of pheochromocytoma are all caused by an excess of circulating catecholamines. The most consistent finding is hypertension, either sustained or paroxysmal, in 80% of patients. Other symptoms include anxiety, palpitations, and tremulousness. The diagnosis is made by demonstrating elevated levels of catecholamines and their metabolites (epinephrine, norepinephrine, metanephrine, and/or vanillylmandelic acid) on a 24-hour urine collection. Cushing's syndrome is associated with refractory hypertension. Other clinical findings include central obesity, proximal weakness, plethora, abdominal stria, hirsutism, and/or hyperpigmentation. The diagnosis is confirmed by hypercortisolism that is not suppressed by low dose steroids (dexamethasone). Renal artery stenosis is characterized by refractory hypertension caused by activation of the renin-angiotensin system secondary to decreased perfusion of the affected kidney. The diagnosis can be difficult, particularly in patients with bilateral disease. Typically, patients have an elevated renal vein renin level. A renal vein renin ratio of greater than or equal to 1.5 (affected vs. non-affected) secures the diagnosis and confirms a hemodynamically significant stenosis. The disease is most commonly seen in the elderly secondary to atherosclerosis. Young women between the ages of 30 and 45 constitute a second population afflicted by this disease. In this group, however, the stenosis is almost invariably secondary to fibromuscular dysplasia.

ANSWER 4

B.

ANSWER 5

E. Duke's staging (Astor–Coller modification)

A2—limited to mucosa

B1—into the muscularis propria

B2—through the muscularis propria

C1—into the muscularis propria with (+) nodes

C2—through the muscularis propria with (+) nodes

This patient has a Duke's B1 tumor. Therefore, no further adjuvant therapy is indicated. Patients with Duke's C tumors (positive lymph nodes) should receive postoperative 5 FU and leucovorin or levamisole. There is argument over whether patients with B2 tumors (tumor invasion through the muscularis propria) should receive adjuvant chemotherapy. Radiation does not play a role in the adjuvant therapy of colon cancer.

ANSWER 6

B. Patients with Duke's B1 tumors have an estimated 5-year survival of 70–85%.

ANSWER 7

C. This patient has a diverticular abscess. Management of this problem has dramatically changed over the past 15 years. First line therapy is now to place a drain in the abscess under CT guidance and admit to the hospital for systemic antibiotics covering gram-negative rods and anaerobes. This initial therapy allows for a trip to the operating room under controlled circumstances after a bowel prep and offers a chance for a one-stage operation, which constitutes resection of the diseased colon and primary anastomosis. A two-stage operation constitutes resection of the diseased colon at the time of operative drainage of the abscess with a Hartman's pouch and end ileostomy, followed by colostomy takedown at a later date. This would be done if percutaneous therapy fails or if the patient presents with peritonitis. A three-stage procedure, now of historical interest only, consisted of drainage of the abscess and diversion, followed by resection of the diseased segment of colon at a second operation and restoration of intestinal continuity at the final operation.

ANSWER 8

E. Answers A through D are all relative indications to proceed with operative management of diverticulitis; however, none require immediate operative intervention. Patients diagnosed at a young age are very likely to have subsequent attacks and suffer complications from them. Failure of non-operative therapy is an indication to proceed with surgery. One must be able to exclude an underlying colon carcinoma. If this is not possible endoscopically, one must proceed with surgery. Patients who have more than one attack are at higher risk to suffer multiple subsequent attacks and therefore are at higher risk for complications (stricture, abscess, fistula, perforation), and it is therefore recommended that those with two or more attacks undergo surgical resection.

ANSWER 9

C. Ulcerative colitis is a disease of unclear etiology that is characterized by abdominal pain and bloody diarrhea. Disease is typically present in the rectum and is confluent without skip areas. It does not affect the small bowel, stomach, or esophagus as opposed to Crohn's disease, which can affect the entire GI tract from mouth to anus. The pathology is limited to the mucosa and submucosa, and therefore bowel wall thickening and fistulas are not characteristic of this disease. Inflammatory pseudopolyps are characteristic. Extraintestinal manifestations, such as erythema nodosum, uveitis, pyoderma gangrenosum, primary sclerosing cholangitis, and arthritis, are common. Colorectal carcinoma is associated with ulcerative colitis with a 1–2% incidence per year, beginning 10 years after initial diagnosis.

ANSWER 10

D. Large bowel obstructions account for only 15% of intestinal obstructions. They are most commonly caused by colorectal carcinoma (65%), diverticulitis (20%), volvulus (5–10%), and miscellaneous causes (10%). Adhesive bands are the most common cause of small bowel obstruction in patients with previous abdominal surgery, but rarely cause large bowel obstruction. Complete large bowel obstruction is a surgical emergency as an intact ileocecal valve makes this a closed loop obstruction, which has an associated high risk of rapid progression to bowel necrosis.

ANSWER 11

A. Adenomatous polyps are divided into tubular, villous, and tubulovillous variants. Approximately 65% of polyps are tubular and these have the lowest (10%) incidence of invasive cancer. Tubulovillous histology accounts for 20% of polyps and 20% harbor cancer. Villous polyps account for 10% of all polyps and have a 25% incidence of carcinoma *in situ* or invasive cancer. The risk of carcinoma increases for all subtypes with increasing polyp size. Hamartomas do not harbor malignancy.

ANSWER 12

D. Vesicoureteral reflux is a common cause of recurrent urinary tract infections in children. Primary reflux is due to muscular ureterotrigonal weakness. Secondary reflux can be due to congenital anomalies such as posterior urethral valves, ectopic ureteral orifices, duplicated ureters, and ureterocele. Other causes include inflammation, neuropathic dysfunction, and iatrogenic injury. The gold standard for diagnosis remains voiding cystourethrography although nuclear scans can make the diagnosis in many cases, and because it is less invasive, it is a reasonable starting point in small children.

ANSWER 13

E. Reflux leads to increased post-void residual volumes of urine that can lead to stasis and bacterial overgrowth. Bacteria are more likely to access the kidney, thus accounting for pyelonephritis. High intravesicular volumes lead to high pressures that are transmitted to the kidney. Stasis associated with reflux can also lead to stone formation. The presence of reflux does not lead to changes in sodium homeostasis.

ANSWER 14

C. Any communication between the bladder and the gastrointestinal tract can cause pneumaturia. Overall, diverticulitis is the most common cause of this phenomenon. The inflammatory process in the left colon causes a fistula between the colon and bladder. Ulcerative colitis does not cause a full thickness lesion and thus does not typically cause fistulas. While Crohn's disease is a full thickness lesion and does predispose to fistulas, it is less common than diverticulitis and a new diagnosis of Crohn's in a 68-year-old is unlikely. Both colon cancer and bladder cancer can lead to fistulas, however, less commonly than diverticular disease. Other evidence of colovesicular fistula includes fecaluria and recurrent urinary tract infections.

ANSWER 15

B. This clinical scenario is characteristic of a ureteral stone. The most common cause of urolithiasis is calcium oxalate, accounting for approximately 70% of all stones. Magnesium ammonium phosphate stones ("struvite") are associated with urinary tract infection caused by organisms that contain the urease enzyme such as *Proteus, Klebsiella,* and *Pseudomonas*. These account for approximately 15% of all ureteral stones. Uric acid stones account for approximately 7% of all stones.

ANSWER 16

A. CT scan is the test of choice for the evaluation of a solid renal mass. In doing so one is attempting to rule in or out renal cell carcinoma. A CT scan can accurately delineate renal cell cancer in over 95% of cases. Angiography typically demonstrates hypervascularity but is only indicated when the CT scan is ambiguous. MRI has promise with regard to preoperative staging of renal cell cancer but is not superior to CT scan and is more expensive. Percutaneous biopsy is contraindicated because the diagnosis can be made without obtaining a tissue diagnosis and seeding of the needle tract with malignant cells during the biopsy is a concern.

ANSWER 17

C.

ANSWER 18

D. Total body water (TBW) is relatively constant for any given person and depends on the amount of fat present within the body. Fat contains little water. TBW as a percent of body weight (BW) decreases with increasing body fat. Estimated TBW in men is 60% of BW and in women is 50% of BW. So, for a 70-kg man ($70 \times 0.60 = 42$ kg), TBW in infants is approximately 80% of BW, decreasing to 65% by 1 year of age. TBW is made up of intracellular fluid (ICF) and extracellular fluid (ECF). ICF is estimated at 2/3 of TBW or 40% BW. ECF is estimated at 30–33% TBW or 20% BW. ECF is made up of intravascular and interstitial spaces. Intravascular space is estimated at 25% of ECF and interstitial spaces are estimated at 25% TBW or 15% of BW.

ANSWER 19

C.

ANSWER 20

A. Sodium (Na) and potassium (K) are the dominant cations in the body. Na is predominantly found in the ECF and in the adult is approximately 60 mEq/kg. The ECF is also made up of small amounts of K, Ca, and Mg. These cations are balanced by Cl anions as well as bicarbonate, phosphorous, sulfate, and anionic proteins in plasma. K is predominantly found in the ICF and is estimated at 42 mEq/kg in the adult. The other cations are Na and Mg, and this is balanced by phosphorous, sulfate, bicarbonate, and anionic proteins. For every 100 mg/dl increase in blood glucose (from normal), serum Na falls 1.5 mEq/L (i.e., $600 - 100 = 500$; $5 \times 1.5 + 8$; $150 - 8 = 142$). Plasma osmolarity is calculated by $(2 \times Na) + (Glucose/18) + (BUN/2.8)$ ($P_{osm} = 2(150) + 600/18 + 12/1.8 = 337$).

ANSWER 21

E. If there is greater than 15 mOsm/L difference between the calculated plasma osmolarity and measured osmolarity then there is an osmolar gap. A gap can be caused by mannitol, ethanol, ethylene glycol, myeloma proteins, or hypertriglyceridemia. The average osmolality is 289 mOsm/kg water.

ANSWER 22

B. Changes in TBW content are reflected by changes in the extracellular solute concentration. Because total body solute content for sodium and potassium remains relatively stable over time, changes in TBW content result in inversely proportional changes in serum sodium. Therefore, abnormalities in serum sodium are an indication of abnormal TBW content. Elevated serum sodium is reflective of decreased TBW content.

ANSWER 23

E. Renin is released from juxtaglomerular cells of the afferent arterioles in response to changes in arterial pressure, changes in sodium delivery to the macula densa of the distal convoluted tubule, increases in beta-adrenergic activity, and increases in cellular cAMP levels.

ANSWER 24

E. Renin released from the juxtaglomerular cells of the kidney cleaves angiotensinogen and alpha2-globulin produced by the liver into angiotensin I. Angiotensin I is then converted to angiotensin II by angiotensin converting enzyme. Angiotensin converting enzyme is produced by vascular endothelial cells and one pass through the pulmonary microvasculature converts most of angiotensin I to angiotensin II. Angiotensin II acts both locally and systemically to increase vascular tone, stimulate catecholamine release from adrenal medulla, affects sodium reabsorption by decreasing renal plasma flow and glomerular filtration coefficient and by direct tubular action and stimulation of aldosterone release from the adrenal cortex.

ANSWER 25

C. Aldosterone is a mineralocorticoid produced within the zona glomerulosa of the adrenal cortex. It increases renal tubular reabsorption of sodium, acting directly on the distal tubular segments, predominantly the collecting tubules. It causes an influx of sodium and causes an increase in Na/K ATPase activity, with a net result of increased sodium reabsorption and increased potassium excretion. The primary regulator of aldosterone secretion is angiotensin II as well as increased potassium, ACTH, and prostaglandins.

ANSWER 26

E. Water loss is divided into sensible (urinary, intestinal, and sweat) and insensible (lungs and skin). Average loss for urine is 800–1500 ml/d with a minimal loss of 300 ml/d. Average insensible loss is 600–900 ml/d, or 8–10 ml/kg/d, with increases of 10% for every degree of body temperature above 37.2°C.

ANSWER 27

B.

ANSWER 28

A.

ANSWER 29

D.

ANSWER 30

D. Factors that place an individual at higher risk of developing breast cancer include:

Family history (including a primary relative with malignancy under age 40, history of bilateral breast cancer, and history of ovarian cancer)

History of previous breast biopsy (regardless of histology)

Nulliparity

BRCA1 positivity—BRCA1 is associated with 5% of all breast cancer. 1/200 women are carriers. BRCA1 is linked to ovarian cancer, is autosomal dominant and has chromosome 17q linkage. Carriers have an 85% lifetime risk of developing cancer. Cystic lesions are not associated with a cancer risk.

Previous personal history of breast cancer

Prior to surgery, patients must have a mammogram to evaluate for multicentric or multifocal disease or a synchronous contralateral tumor. BRCA1 genetics is a screening tool for high-risk populations and is not used once a mass is present or for general population screening. Factors that help predict recurrence include: tumor size, histologic grading, ER and PR status, and flow cytometry. Controversial factors include Her-2/neu and cathepsin D. Patient age does not predict recurrence. This patient has a tumor greater than 5 cm and (+) ipsilateral axillary nodes; therefore she is Stage IIIa.

TNM staging of breast cancer

Tis-tumor *in situ*

T1- <2 cm

T2- >2 cm but <5 cm

T3- >5 cm

T4- any size with extension into skin or chest wall

N0- (−) nodes

N1- (+) ipsilateral axillary nodes

N2- (+) fixed positive ipsilateral axillary nodes

N3- (+) ipsilateral internal mammary nodes

M0- no metastasis

M1- distant metastasis

Stage	T	N	M
Stage 0	Tis	N0	M0
Stage I	T1	N0	M0
Stage IIa	T0	N1	M0
	T1	N0	M0
	T2	N0	M0
Stage IIb	T2	N1	M0
	T3	N0	M0
Stage IIIa	T0	N2	M0
	T1	N2	M0
	T2	N2	M0
	T3	N1,2	M0
Stage IIIb	T4	Any N	M0
	Any T	N3	M0
Stage IV	Any T	Any N	M1

ANSWER 31

A. Characteristics on mammogram that are suspicious for malignancy include: densities with irregular margins, spiculated lesions, microcalcifications, or rod-like or branching patterns.

ANSWER 32

C. The most likely diagnosis is fibrocystic change, which is characterized by palpable painful masses, which fluctuate in size with the menstrual cycle. The symptoms may become worse with advancing age until menopause when the symptoms cease. Fibrocystic change is a normal condition but it does carry a 1.5- to 11-fold increased risk of subsequent cancer. The other choices are all benign breast disorders.

ANSWER 33

D. Gynecomastia is normal in puberty and aging. Things that can cause gynecomastia include excess estrogen, deficient androgens, and drug side effects. Drugs that can cause gynecomastia can be split into four groups:

1) **drugs with estrogen activity** (anabolic steroids, clomiphene citrate, diethylpropion hydrochloride, diethylstilbestrol, digitalis, estrogens, heroin, oral contraceptives, cannabis)

2) **drugs that inhibit the action/synthesis of testosterone** (antineoplastic agents, d-pencillamine, diazepam, flutamide, ketoconazole, medroxyprogesterone acetate, phenytoin, spironolactone)

3) **drugs that enhance estrogen synthesis by the testis** (human chorionic gonadotropin)

4) **drugs with an unknown mechanism** (amiodarone, bumetanide, busulfan, domperidone, ethionamide, furosemide, isoniazid, methyldopa, nifedipine, reserpine, sulindac, theophylline, tricyclic antidepressants, verapamil)

ANSWER 34

B. The internal mammary nodes drain all four quadrants of the breast. The level of axillary lymph nodes is based on the nodes relationship to the pectoralis minor. Level one nodes are lateral to the muscle, level two nodes are beneath the muscle, and level three nodes are medial to the muscle.

ANSWER 35

B. There are two critical motor nerves to be aware of while performing a mastectomy or axillary dissection. The thoracodorsal nerve provides motor function to the latissimus dorsi and damage causes weakness in shoulder abduction. The long thoracic nerve provides motor function to the serratus anterior and damage causes a winged scapula.

ANSWER 36

C. Bleomycin is an anti-tumor antibody with renal excretion that has associated dose related pulmonary fibrosis.

ANSWER 37

B. Cis-platinum is a platinum coordination compound, also with renal excretion.

ANSWER 38

A. Taxol is a mitotic spindle inhibitor used in the treatment of breast cancer.

ANSWER 39

D. Tamoxifen is a nonsteroidal antiestrogen, also used for the treatment of breast cancer.

ANSWER 40

B. Gallstones are composed of bile salts, lecithin, and cholesterol. Varying concentrations of these components characterize the classification of gallstones. Pigmented stones have a high concentration of bile salts and a low concentration of cholesterol. Cholesterol calculi are composed of a high concentration of cholesterol and a low concentration of bile salts. Pigmented gallstones are the most common stones seen worldwide while cholesterol gallstones are the most common form found in the United States.

ANSWER 41

B.

ANSWER 42

B. This patient presents with primary sclerosing cholangitis, which is an idiopathic disease of the biliary tree. 60% of cases of PSC occur in patients with ulcerative colitis, and the risk for PSC remains even after colectomy. Pancreatitis and diabetes mellitus are also associated with this disease but at a much lower frequency. This disease causes multiple intra and extra hepatic strictures of the bile ducts and is best diagnosed by ERCP that documents multiple strictures and dilatations (beading) of the bile ducts.

ANSWER 43

A.

ANSWER 44

A. Emphysematous cholecystitis is a potentially lethal complication of cholecystitis. Radiographic images show gas within the gallbladder lumen and wall. *Clostridium perfringens* is the most common organism cultured. Emergent cholecystectomy is warranted for this condition secondary to the associated high morbidity and mortality when left untreated.

ANSWER 45

D.

ANSWER 46

A. According to current data, less than 10% of patients with asymptomatic gallstones develop significant symptoms over a 5-year period and because of this almost all cases of asymptomatic gallstones are simply followed. Chenodeoxycholic acid has a success rate of complete stone dissolution of only 13.5% when used in high doses and a high rate of relapse upon cessation of therapy. Percutaneous transhepatic cholecystolitholysis requires intubation of the biliary tree and instillation of an agent that dissolves cholesterol. Patients with symptomatic stones should, in general, undergo cholecystectomy to avoid complications of stones such as cholecystitis, choledocholithiasis, pancreatitis, or cholangitis.

ANSWER 47

D. "Giant" congenital nevus is one that is of sufficient size to cover the particular regional anatomy. For example, a nevus covering an entire upper eyelid or nose is considered just as large as one the size of a bathing suit. The critical histologic distinction between giant nevi and congenital nevi is that giant nevi typically contain cells going in single file into the deeper dermis and they involve adnexal structures. They also may contain lymphocytic infiltrates and neural structures. The actual incidence of malignant change is 1–2%. The malignant change is most often melanoma. Undifferentiated neural tumors can also occur. A good approach to these nevi is to discuss the risks with the parents and convey that the decision to proceed with excision is usually based on cosmetics, but be quick to biopsy any area of pigment change, increased nodularity within the tumor, or overt malignant changes.

ANSWER 48

C. Seborrheic keratosis is benign and localized to the superficial dermis. There are usually multiple lesions present and are elevated, dark black, with a waxy, creased surface. It is recommended to perform an excisional biopsy on one of these lesions to confirm the diagnosis and then you can shave these and cauterize the base to destroy remaining cells in the basal layer of the epidermis.

ANSWER 49

D. The most common non-pigmented skin lesions are benign and either age-related or sun-induced. Age-related lesions are papillomas, or skin-tags. They are never malignant and can usually be excised without any further treatment. Sun-induced lesions are actinic keratoses. These are usually pink, scaly lesions, which then become hyperkeratotic. Approximately 1/1,000 progress to squamous carcinoma, but up to 25% may spontaneously regress. There are several variants of actinic keratosis. Bowen's disease is squamous cell carcinoma *in situ*, which usually consists of larger plaques in non-sun exposed areas. Bowen's disease is not associated with an increased risk of internal malignancies. A hypertrophic variety exists that grow out as a firm spike, or cutaneous horn. These can develop squamous cell carcinoma at their base. Increased growth ulceration, or recurrent crusting in one of these lesions is sufficient reason for excisional biopsy. Multiple lesions can be treated with topical fluorouracil after biopsy confirms diagnosis.

ANSWER 50

C. Up to 65% of cancers in the United States are basal and squamous cell carcinomas. The ratio of basal cell to squamous cell carcinoma is about 5:1, with men affected more than women. Sun-exposed areas are at the highest risk. There are no precursors to basal cell carcinoma. Precursors to squamous cell carcinoma include: actinic keratoses, Bowen's disease, and cutaneous horn. Both cancers are in most cases secondary to UVB radiation. Other risk factors include: older age, male sex, skin that burns or tans easily, Celtic ancestry, fair hair and freckles, sun exposure, ionizing radiation, arsenic exposure, xeroderma pigmentosum, basal cell nevus syndrome, albinism, skin cancer, burn scars, immunosuppression, chronic ulcers. Treatment consists of excisional biopsy with clear margins.

BLOCK TWO

ANSWERS

ANSWER 51

E. Patients with a family history of dysplastic nevi have an increased risk of developing melanoma. Dysplastic nevi are frequently variegated, have fuzzy borders, and generally measure greater than 5-mm in diameter. A target shape or "fried egg" pattern is classic for dysplastic nevi. Patients with dysplastic nevi should be followed closely. Photographs are helpful in following dysplastic nevi. Any suspicious dysplastic nevus should be biopsied. It is not necessary to excise all dysplastic nevi.

ANSWER 52

B. Peptic ulcer disease is the most frequent cause of upper GI bleeding. This consists of both duodenal ulcers (25%) and gastric ulcers (20%). Other causes include Mallory–Weiss tears (10%), which occurs after retching or vomiting and is usually self-limited and esophageal varices (20%) secondary to portal hypertension, gastritis (20%), and sporadic rare causes (5%).

ANSWER 53

A. This patient has an actively bleeding ulcer. Often this can be controlled with endoscopic techniques; however, when this fails one must be prepared to proceed urgently to the operating room to control the bleeding. An urgent procedure for bleeding should not be explored with laparoscopy. Admission to the ICU is inappropriate.

ANSWER 54

C. This patient is hemodynamically stable. No heroic maneuvers like clamping the aorta are necessary. Vascular control is obtained by opening the duodenum and placing sutures in the base of the ulcer to ligate the gastroduodenal artery and its branches. One does not need to and should not endeavor to visualize the artery.

ANSWER 55

A. The patient has presented with painless jaundice and weight loss, which must be considered a periampullary tumor until proven otherwise. CT scan is the test of choice in the initial evaluation of a suspected pancreatic mass. It can document the presence of the mass as well as determine the extent of disease and resectability.

ANSWER 56

A. The most favorable prognosis occurs with ampullary adenocarcinoma, which carries a 36% 5-year survival after resection. This is followed by distal bile duct tumors with a 34% 5-year survival, periampullary duodenum with a 33% 5-year survival and finally pancreatic adenocarcinoma with an 18% 5-year survival. Each lesion is typically treated with a pancreaticoduodenectomy (Whipple procedure).

ANSWER 57

D. Nitrates and their reactive metabolites, nitrites, have been linked to gastric cancer, but not pancreatic cancer. Each of the other substances has been linked to pancreatic carcinoma. However, because each only marginally increases risk and the incidence of pancreatic cancer is low, screening programs for this disease are not helpful.

ANSWER 58

B. This patient presented with "Whipple's triad" (hypoglycemic symptoms that improve with intravenous glucose and a fasting glucose <50) suggesting an insulinoma, which is a malignancy of the pancreatic beta cell. Alpha cells produce glucagon. Glucagonomas are often larger at diagnosis than other islet cell tumors, and the clinical syndrome consists of mild diabetes with necrolytic migratory erythema. Malnutrition and weight loss are also often seen. D cells produce somatostatin and can form somatostatinomas. These are among the most rare pancreatic neoplasms. They produce severe hyperglycemia, diarrhea, and cholelithiasis.

ANSWER 59

E. This patient has acute pancreatitis. Ranson's criteria are a set of values, five of which are obtained on admission and six others at 48 hours after admission, that provide prognostic information. This patient has 10 of 11 criteria present (all except low calcium) and therefore the best estimate of his mortality is 100%. In general, the estimated mortality is as follows:

0–2 criteria	0% mortality
3–4	15%
5–6	50%
>7	100%

ANSWER 60

B. Posterior hip dislocations are the most common dislocation, 75% of which occur as a result of a motor vehicle crash. If no associated hip fracture exists, the leg will be internally rotated and there can be a palpable posterior fullness. Anterior dislocations are externally rotated with an anterior fullness. Initial treatment consists of emergent closed reduction to avoid avascular necrosis of the femoral head that occurs with 15% of posterior dislocations and 5% of anterior injuries.

ANSWER 61

E. There are a tremendous number of conditions that can cause hypercalcemia. The most common cause in hospitalized patients is malignancy (breast cancer, metastases to bone, multiple myeloma, leukemia, PTH-rp secreting tumors (lung)). Endocrine disorders such as hyperparathyroidism, hyperthyroidism, and Addison's disease can also cause hypercalcemia. Increased calcium intake with disorders such as milk–alkali syndrome, vitamin A and D intoxication, and drugs, such as thiazide, diuretics, and lithium, are also implicated. Granulomatous diseases, such as tuberculosis and sarcoid, likewise can (rarely) cause hypercalcemia.

ANSWER 62

E. This patient has symptomatic hypercalcemia with an inappropriately elevated PTH level, therefore securing the diagnosis of primary hyperparathyroidism which necessitates surgical therapy. The most common cause of primary hyperparathyroidism is parathyroid adenoma (80%), hyperplasia (20%), and carcinoma (<1%). Whether or not to obtain preoperative imaging studies remains an area of great controversy; however, it is acceptable to simply proceed to neck exploration without any further radiologic studies.

ANSWER 63

E. Groin hernias are more common in men and in Caucasians and are more frequently right-sided. They present with incarceration in approximately 10% of cases and are common in children. Hernias do not resolve spontaneously but rather get larger with time and can cause complications such as bowel obstruction, incarceration, and strangulation, and should therefore, in general, be surgically repaired.

ANSWER 64

B.

ANSWER 65

A.

ANSWER 66

E.

ANSWER 67

C.

ANSWER 68

D.

ANSWER 69

D. There are four histologic subtypes of melanoma: superficial spreading (70%), acral lentiginous (5%), nodular (15–30%), and lentigo maligna (4–10%). It typically arises in a pre-existing mole. Characteristics that should raise your concern for melanoma in a mole include **A**ssymetry, **B**order irregularity, **C**olor variation, and **D**iameter >6 mm. Stage is determined by depth of the primary lesion (Breslow scale), with tumors less than 0.75 mm having a cure rate of approximately 95% with excision alone.

ANSWER 70

D.

ANSWER 71

A.

ANSWER 72

A. Barium swallow is the first diagnostic procedure obtained when a patient presents with the symptom of dysphagia. Otherwise, an EGD is the first diagnostic procedure obtained for symptoms of esophageal disease. Barrett's esophagus presents as tongue-like extensions of epithelium extending up from the GE junction. Candida esophagitis usually involves the entire esophagus, with more extensive disease in the proximal esophagus. A Mallory–Weiss tear appears as a discrete laceration at the GE junction and gastric carcinoma presents more commonly as an extension of the disease from the stomach. Initial therapy for Barrett's esophagus is acid suppression with an H-2 blocker or proton pump inhibitor. The goal is to prevent acid reflux in order to prevent further stimulus for Barrett's metaplasia. This is a premalignant lesion. Serial surveillance endoscopy and biopsy must be performed to ensure that there are no foci of high grade dysplasia or carcinoma *in situ*, which would require more aggressive therapy (esophagectomy). Surgical therapy for acid reflux/Barrett's is a Nissen fundoplication, which obviates the need for long-term pharmacologic therapy.

ANSWER 73

C.

ANSWER 74

C. The absence of peristalsis and failure of relaxation of the lower esophageal sphincter (LES) on esophageal manometry is diagnostic of achalasia. The barium swallow shows the classic "bird's beak" sign which manifested by the nonrelaxation of the LES with progressive esophageal dilation. The LES in patients with diffuse esophageal spasm has a normal resting pressure and relaxes with deglutition. Nutcracker esophagus is characterized by prolonged high amplitude waves on esophageal manometry. Patients with GERD typically have normal esophageal motility. Patients with abnormal motility should not undergo Nissen fundoplication as the fundoplication will likely exacerbate their motility disorder. Achalasia is treated by Heller myotomy, which divides the circular muscle of the LES allowing passage of a food bolus into the stomach. Medical treatments utilizing botulinum toxin injections or calcium channel blockers have shown some promise but require continuous therapy and usually result in transient improvement at best.

ANSWER 75

D.

ANSWER 76

E. Ingestion of caustic materials is common in children. Liquid alkali is usually swallowed quickly and most often does not damage the mouth or oropharynx. Therefore, ingestion cannot be ruled out by evaluation of the oral cavity. Vomiting or dilution should not be attempted as this worsens the injury. Airway compromise is common and initial observation is critical. Both esophagraphy and EGD are needed to assess the extent of injury and strictures as well as carcinoma which may occur with healing of the esophageal epithelium.

ANSWER 77

D. Boerhaave's syndrome is perforation of the esophagus after extensive vomiting and retching and is not associated with esophageal cancer. Plummer–Vinson syndrome is a premalignant condition typically seen in elderly women who are edentulous and have atrophic oral mucosa, glossitis, and koilonychia. Caustic strictures carry an increased risk of subsequent malignancy, often many years after the injury. This requires long-term surveillance. Barrett's esophagus also carries a risk of malignancy. The area of metaplastic change must be routinely surveyed with endoscopic biopsies to look for areas of dysplasia. High-grade dysplasia carries the highest risk of cancer and may warrant surgical resection if it is documented.

ANSWER 78

A. The DCC mutation is found in colon cancer and has no role in esophageal diverticula or carcinoma. While all the remaining answers can lead to diverticula, most diverticula are caused by elevated intraluminal pressures. Elevated pressures cause the mucosa and submucosa to herniate through the muscular wall of the esophagus. These are known as pulsion diverticula and are often associated with motor disorders of the esophagus.

ANSWER 79

E. All the organisms listed are associated with infectious esophagitis. However, *Candida albicans* is the most common organism associated with esophagitis. This patient is particularly susceptible to infectious esophagitis, particularly *Candida*, because of his immunocompromised state, secondary to anti-rejection medications. Syphilitic and tubercular esophagitis are rare. The second most common source of infectious esophagitis is viral, with HSV being the most common in immunosuppressed patients and CMV the most common in HIV patients.

ANSWER 80

B. You assist the patient's breathing with bag and mask ventilation without difficulty. Her oxygen saturation improves to 99%, and her heart rate normalizes.

ANSWER 81

D.

ANSWER 82

B. This patient was hypoxic following routine surgery. Her arterial blood gas is consistent with an uncompensated respiratory acidosis. The most common cause of postoperative hypoxia/hypoventilation is over sedation. Evidence of abdominal perforation would not present in such a short period of time. While emergent reintubation should always be considered, oxygenation and ventilation established by bag and mask is adequate while treating over sedation. Naloxone is a competitive inhibitor of the morphine receptors that inhibit spontaneous respiration in the central nervous system. While most patients will automatically ventilate the excess CO_2 obtained from abdominal insufflation, with central respiratory arrest, this will not occur. Even short periods of hypoxia can cause myocardial ischemia and infarction in the elderly that is confirmed on EKG. The chest x-ray in this scenario shows air under the diaphragm that is to be expected after laparoscopic surgery. In instances where surgery has not just occurred, this sign would be abnormal.

ANSWER 83

B.

ANSWER 84

C.

ANSWER 85

D. This patient has pulmonary artery catheter numbers consistent with septic shock. This is supported by a low SVR and high cardiac index. The initial treatment would be to attempt to improve preload and therefore assist in systemic perfusion. Dopamine or other peripheral vasoconstrictors may be required as an adjunct to optimizing intravascular volume. However, vasoconstriction in the face of hypovolemia is detrimental to systemic perfusion as well as cardiac work. A beta-blocker is contraindicated. The patient's tachycardia and hypotension are not secondary to a poorly functioning ventricle. Rather, the patient's cardiac system is attempting to improve systemic perfusion. The diagnostic tests obtained show no evidence of pulmonary disease. Troponin levels are within normal limits making a postoperative infarction unlikely. The abdominal ultrasound shows a markedly dilated gallbladder wall with pericholecystic fluid. HIDA can show no filling of the gallbladder, which is consistent with acalculous cholecystitis (AC). AC occurs in as much as 1% of postoperative cardiac patients and is a feared complication in the surgical intensive care unit due to its occult nature and its resultant significant morbidity. Current theories suggest that relative hypotension during cardiopulmonary bypass leads to ischemia and necrosis of the gallbladder wall. Other acutely ill ICU patients can also develop AC.

ANSWER 86

C. In general, enteral nutrition is favored over other types of nutrition. It prevents atrophy of the gut mucosa and may have fewer associated complications than total parenteral nutrition, particularly infectious complications. Critically ill patients are tremendously catabolic, and enteral nutrition should be started early after surgery. Maintenance IV fluids do not meet caloric requirements for critically ill patients. Parenertal nutrition is used with patients who do not have a functioning GI tract. The most common complication from parental nutrition is infection of the central line into which it is infusing.

ANSWER 87

A., E.

ANSWER 88

B.

ANSWER 89

C.

ANSWER 90

C. The two major means by which to increase pO_2 are increasing PEEP or FiO_2. Adding an inspiratory pause or changing the tidal volume has no effect on oxygenation. PCO_2 is best decreased by either increasing tidal volume or increasing respiratory rate. Dead space ventilation (the volume of air within the tracheobronchial tree) does not undergo gas exchange. Dead space ventilation will not change with a change in tidal volume over time but will dramatically increase with a change in respiratory rate over time. Therefore, the most efficient way to blow off this patient's CO_2 is to increase the tidal volume. The proper position of the endotracheal tube on the chest x-ray is 1–2 cm above the carina. Beyond this location leads to right main stem intubation and above this position can lead to accidental extubation and inefficient ventilation.

ANSWER 91

E. Actions of thyroid hormones include: 1) Development: essential for normal neural and skeletal development; calorigenesis, increased oxygen consumption, increased basal metabolic rate. 2) Intermediary metabolism: increased protein synthesis, increased synthesis/degradation of cholesterol, increased lipolysis, increased glycogenolysis and gluconeogenesis. 3) Cardiovascular: increased heart rate and myocardial contractility. 4) Sympathetic nervous system: increased sensitivity to catecholamines, increased catecholamine receptors in cardiac muscle, amplification of catechol effects at other sites. 5) Endocrine: increased steroid hormone release. 6) Hematopoietic: increased erythropoiesis, increased 2,3 DPG production. 7) Respiratory: maintains hypoxic and hypercapnic drive. 8) Musculoskeletal: increased bone turnover, increased urinary hydroxyproline excretion, increased rate of muscle relaxation.

ANSWER 92

B. C cells of thyroid and multiple other organs secrete calcitonin. It is a potent inhibitor of osteoclastic bone resorption and enhances renal calcium excretion.

ANSWER 93

B. Causes of hypothyroidism include: 1) Thyroiditis—Hashimoto's, viral, Reidel's. 2) Prior I^{131}. 3) Prior surgery. 4) Iodine excess (Wolff–Chaikoff effect). 5) Iodine deficiency. 6) Thyroid hormone resistance. 7) Colloid goiter.

ANSWER 94

A. The management of a definitively benign thyroid mass is TSH suppression. Indications for thyroidectomy include:

Benign 1) Multinodular goiter with compression or symptoms. 2) Large single nodule with compression or symptoms. 3) Thyrotoxicosis: Graves' disease, Plummer's disease, toxic nodule.

Indeterminate 1) Follicular adenoma with atypical cells on FNA. 2) Hürthle cell tumor. 3) Capillary hemangioma. 4) Premalignant states: MEN-II patients, familial medullary (RET proto-oncogene).

Malignant 1) Carcinoma: papillary, follicular, medullary, anaplastic.

ANSWER 95

A. Arterial supply to the thyroid is derived from the superior thyroid artery (external carotid), inferior thyroid artery (thyrocervical trunk from the subclavian artery), and in some patients the thyroid ima. Venous drainage is accomplished with bilateral superior, middle, and inferior thyroid veins all of which drain into the respective internal jugular vein. The right recurrent laryngeal nerve loops around the subclavian and the left loops around the aortic arch. The risk of injury to the recurrent laryngeal nerve is 5%.

ANSWER 96

D. Differential diagnosis of hypercalcemia includes: primary hyperparathyroidism, tertiary hyperparathyroidism, familial hypercalcemic hypocalcuria, paraneoplastic syndrome, osteolytic metastases, multiple myeloma, drug induced hypercalcemia, granulomatous disease, hypervitaminosis D, milk–alkali syndrome, immobilization, and idiopathic.

ANSWER 97

A. Symptoms of hyperparathyroidism include: renal—calculi, nephrocalcinosis, polyuria, nocturia; musculoskeletal—muscle weakness, calcific tendonitis, chondrocalcinosis, osteitis fibrosa cystica (brown tumors); gastrointestinal—anorexia, nausea, vomiting, dyspepsia, constipation; CNS—impaired mentation, loss of recent memory, lethargy, insomnia, emotional lability, depression, worsening of pre-existing CNS or psychological disorders, somnolence, coma; skin—pruritus; eye—band keratopathy; cardiovascular—hypertension and heart block. The actions of PTH include: Kidney—increased calcium reabsorption, decreased phosphate and bicarbonate reabsorption (the 1–34 sequence activates an intracellular protein kinase C pathway to induce calcium reabsorption and phosphate excretion), converts 25, (OH) Vit D3 to 1,25, (OH) 2 Vit D3 (the initial 2 amino acids of sequence 1–34 signal activation of an adenyl cyclase Gs protein, then 2–27 as a minimum results in an increase in 1 alpha hydroxylation of 23, monohydroxyl Vit D); bone—increased osteoclastic activity, decreased osteoblastic activity, increased rapid phase calcium mobilization, increased bone resorption, increased phosphate resorption. PTH secretion is controlled by calcium, vitamin D3, and magnesium.

ANSWER 98

A. When working up primary hyperparathyroidism you must check serum calcium and a PTH. Other studies that may be checked during the workup include a 24-hour urinary calcium, calcium/creatinine clearance ratio (urine Ca X serum Creat/serum Ca X urine Creat) should be >0.01 to rule out FHH, and bone densitometry.

ANSWER 99

B. Multiple Endocrine Neoplasia—Type I

Dominant inheritance, hyperplastic glands in all affected patients—hyperplasia of supranumary glands—usually severe hyperparathyroidism; other features: gastrinoma, pituitary neoplasms, ovarian, adrenal, carcinoid tumors.

Multiple Endocrine Neoplasia—Type II

MEN II is characterized by autosomal dominant inheritance. MEN IIA and MEN IIB share the common features of medullary carcinoma of the thyroid and pheochromocytoma. The third aspect of IIA is parathyroid hyperplasia. The third aspect of characterizing IIB is mucosal neuromas.

ANSWER 100

A.

ANSWER 101

B. This patient has a classic history and physical exam for acute appendicitis. No further tests are indicated, particularly with a young man. One should proceed directly to appendectomy.